Following the Shaman's Path

A Walking Guide to Little Petroglyph Canyon, Coso Range, California

David S. Whitley

MATURANGO MUSEUM

Museum Administrator .... .Richard Senn

Curator .... Elva Younkin

Set up and published by the Maturango Press
for the
MATURANGO MUSEUM
of Indian Wells Valley, Ridgecrest, CA.

First Printing, May 1998

Coordinating Editors, **Jean M. Bennett & Elva Younkin**

Book & Cover design by **Olivia V. Francis**

Cover photograph by **Mark Pahuta**

A panel from Little Petroglyph Canyon
in the Coso Range, Inyo County, CA

MATURANGO MUSEUM PUBLICATION NO. 13

ISBN 0-943-041-06-6

TABLE OF CONTENTS

▼

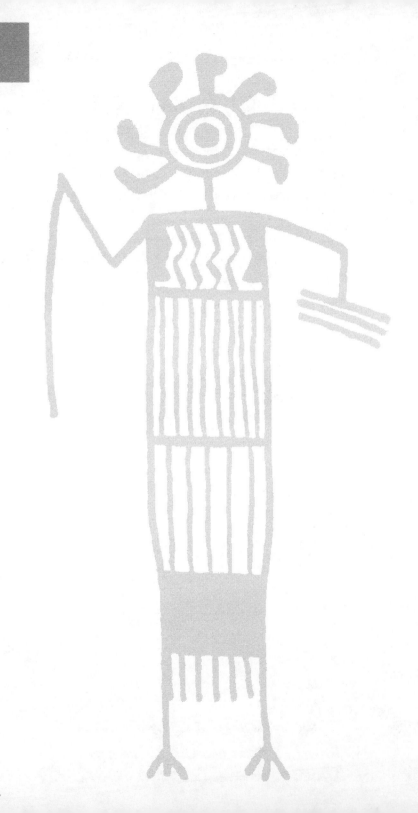

ACKNOWLEDGEMENTS

This guide represents an effort to make the results of twenty years of archaeological research accessible to the non-archaeologist. I have incurred many debts over the years in getting to the point where this guide could be completed. On the research side I am particularly grateful to Ron Dorn, with whom I have conducted dating research on Mojave Desert petroglyphs since 1981, and Joe Simon, who accompanied me on my first Coso study in 1978 and has been with me seemingly ever since. I was greatly aided in the preparation of this guide by a number of individuals at the Maturango Museum who kindly read over the manuscript and field-checked it in Little Petroglyph Canyon. I thank Judy Breitenstein, Dave Ganger, Charlotte and Don Goodson, Mike and Jean King, Bruce Wertenberger, and Al Woodman for their assistance. I also thank Jean Bennett and Elva Younkin, both of whom have provided help and support in innumerable ways, and without whose assistance this project (like many others) couldn't have been completed. Finally, I would like to thank the Commander of the China Lake Naval Air Weapons Station, who has provided me with permission over the years to conduct research on the Coso petroglyphs; and his staff, particularly Peggy Shoaf and Raymond Kelso, both of whom have been exceptionally helpful in different but equally important ways.

I

INTRODUCTION TO
THE COSO PETROGLYPHS

Little Petroglyph Canyon is a national treasure. Located in the Coso Mountains of eastern California, it is part of one of the largest concentrations of rock art in North America, and it stands as a permanent testimony to the artistry, symbolism and religious beliefs of our Native American forebears. The geographical remoteness of Little Petroglyph Canyon, in the high reaches of rugged volcanic badlands, has for many years helped separate this rock art from our modern lives. Distant from our everyday activities, the art has also seemed far removed from us intellectually and culturally. Hard to see, and harder still to know and understand, the petroglyphs are a remote enigma that, like a lost city, can only be reached and understood with great effort.

In recent years archaeologists have begun to unravel the mystery of the Coso petroglyphs. New and sophisticated scientific techniques have allowed the dating of these rock engravings for the first time, giving us information about the antiquity of this art. Using historical records and accounts of the Native American inhabitants of this region, archaeologists have also begun to reconstruct the rituals and symbolism of the petroglyphs, showing that they were tied to the shaman and his vision quests. And, by studying the neuropsychology of the human mind, they are now identifying the universal aspects of these petroglyphs, finding the characteristics that are common to all humans and showing that, instead of being enigmatic, the petroglyphs are part of a wider phenomenon reflecting the origins of human creativity and religious beliefs.

This walking guide is intended to lead you through Little Petroglyph Canyon and to help you understand the art preserved in the Cosos. It begins with a brief background discussion that answers some of a visitor's most common questions about this art. It then will move you down the canyon, identifying, describing and explaining a selected set of the panels of art. These panels, and the discussions of them, will help you understand the remainder of the art in this magnificent canyon, as well as the rock art in the Mojave Desert, eastern California and Nevada more generally. The panels will also serve to illustrate — as they were originally intended — the beliefs and practices of the Native American shamans-artists, revealing the complex religious symbolism of our Native American forebears.

▼ Visiting the Petroglyphs

The Coso petroglyphs are located within the China Lake Naval Air Weapons Station, outside of Ridgecrest, California. This location within a military facility has served to preserve and protect the Coso sites, and the Navy deserves a strong vote of thanks for their care of the sites. But this also necessarily makes access to them more difficult. The Navy has made arrangements so that Little Petroglyph Canyon, the biggest and most spectacular of the Coso sites, may be visited on tours run by the Maturango Museum, 100 East Las Flores Avenue, Ridgecrest, CA 93555; phone 760-375-6900; FAX 760-375-0479 (email: matmus@ridgecrest.ca.us). These tours are conducted on weekends during the spring and fall and are often booked-up long in advance, so make your reservations early.

Although the museum tours provide you with an introduction to the petroglyphs, once you are in the canyon you will be able to move up and down the canyon at your own pace. Though guides will be spaced throughout the canyon to help you, this booklet is intended to provide the information you need, working on your own, to understand and appreciate this art.

▼ Common Questions About the Petroglyphs

Most visitors share certain general questions about the petroglyphs that may be answered without reference to a specific motif or panel. The discussion below answers many of these questions and provides an introduction to understanding the rock art once you are in the canyon.

▼ Rock art was either pecked with a hammerstone or painted with mineral earths.

The two most common kinds of rock art are pictographs, or rock paintings, and petroglyphs, or rock engravings. Pictographs were created with paints made by mixing ground mineral earths (like ocher or kaolin) or charcoal with a liquid, such as animal blood or water. These paints were applied with the fingers or with a brush made from the tip of a tail of a small animal. Petroglyphs were made with a stone cobble, using this to hammer through the dark coating of rock varnish on the outside of the rock, to create a design in the lighter heart rock exposed below. The rock art in the Cosos is primarily but not exclusively petroglyphs. We refer to the individual pictograph and petroglyph designs as motifs, with the grouping of motifs on a rock face called a panel.

▼ Coso petroglyphs were made by Shoshone and Paiute speaking people.

During the historical period, the Coso region was occupied by peoples speaking one of three different Numic languages: Shoshone, Southern Paiute, and Northern Paiute. The Coso Shoshone were the primary occupants of the Coso Mountains but the Southern Paiute-speaking Kawaiisu lived along its southern edge and the Northern Paiute occupied Owens Valley, immediately to the north. Historical accounts indicate that all three of these different groups used the Cosos for rituals, and we believe that all three were responsible for making its rock art.

Although we cannot be certain, historical linguistics and archaeological evidence suggest that these Numic speakers occupied the Coso region for thousands of years. It is reasonable to assume that older rock art was also made by the ancestors of these same historic peoples.

▼ Shamans made the petroglyphs.

Our historical records indicate that petroglyphs were made by one particular group: shamans or medicine men. These were healers and religious and political leaders who were believed to be able to go into the supernatural world by entering a trance. They did this primarily to acquire supernatural power, which they usually obtained in the form of an animal spirit helper. But they also entered the supernatural and used its powers to cure, make rain, control animals, find lost objects, predict the future and, sometimes, bewitch their enemies. Among the Numic-speaking peoples, shamans were primarily older men.

Supernatural power was called *poha*. A shaman was known as a *pohagunt*, or "man having power". Rock art sites were among the most powerful of the ritual locations used by shamans. They were called *pohaghani*, or "house of power".

▼ Petroglyphs were made at the conclusion of the shaman's vision quest.

Petroglyphs were made at the conclusion of the shaman's vision quest, immediately after he came out of his trance. This vision quest involved isolation from other people, fasting, meditation and, sometimes, the use of tobacco. All of these activities can result in hallucinations, which were considered to be sacred visions.

Rock art sites then were vision quest sites. Vision quests were sometimes conducted at remote locations, including sites that were great distances from a shaman's home village. But they also might be completed in the rocks surrounding this same village, reflecting the fact that Native Americans viewed all locations as potentially sacred. When vision quests were undertaken near a village, this occurred during the season when the village inhabitants had moved on to another temporary location. The vision quest and the making of rock art were solitary rituals of the shaman.

▼ Petroglyphs portray the visionary imagery of the shaman's trance.

In general terms, the petroglyphs depict the visionary images and hallucinatory events of the shaman while in his trance. They were a record of his sacred experiences, and they allow us to see today how the shamans of the past viewed their sacred realm. Shamans, however, conducted vision quests and entered trances for different reasons. Some petroglyphs may depict spirit helpers or other supernatural beings, others may portray the shaman as he thought he looked while in the supernatural realm, and still others may have been intended to portray the shaman making rain while in the supernatural realm, bewitching his opponents, and so on. And, as we shall see, many petroglyphs simply illustrate *poha*, or supernatural power, in an abstract form.

▼ Petroglyphs were made to permanently record the shaman's vision.

There were probably many reasons for making the petroglyphs: social, cultural, and so on. On one level the shaman engraved this art simply to demonstrate that he had experienced the supernatural, and to permanently proclaim his resulting religious position and importance for anyone to see. But on another level we also know that, during trances, our short-term memory is impaired and we easily forget what we have just experienced, because of changes in our brain chemistry. (The same chemical changes occur while we are sleeping, which is why most people do not remember their dreams.) To forget the visions and lose the power bestowed by the supernatural experience was believed to cause sickness or even death, so that shamans were very concerned with remembering these sacred events. They made petroglyphs to permanently record their visions, and sometimes used them later in life to revitalize their supernatural experiences.

▼ Bighorn sheep petroglyphs represent the Rain-shaman's spirit helper.

The most common petroglyph in the Cosos is the bighorn sheep. Visions of bighorn sheep spirits were believed to yield rainmaking power because bighorns were the special spirit helpers of the Rain-shaman. The large numbers of bighorn petroglyphs in the Cosos reflect the belief that it was the best location throughout the Numic speaking region to obtain rainmaking power. Historical accounts indicate that shamans came from as far as northeastern Utah to the Cosos for these rituals.

Because the association of a shaman with his spirit helper was so great, he was believed to sometimes transform into his animal spirit when he went into the supernatural. Some "bighorns" are shown as combinations of human and animal features, and some of the bighorn motifs portray the internal body design that is also seen in many of the human figures, signaling this equivalence between shaman and helper.

Other animal petroglyphs portray other spirit helpers.

Most animal motifs probably portray spirit helpers of different kinds, who could provide the shaman with a miscellany of general powers. Rattlesnakes, often shown just as a zigzag line (mimicking the path of a sidewinder), are common and were the special spirit helpers of Rattlesnake-shamans, who could cure snake bites. Coyotes, however, were not spirit helpers but were believed to be evil spirits that could be sent from the supernatural to bewitch an enemy.

Human figures portray the shaman and other spirits in the supernatural realm.

Native American accounts indicate that most of the human motifs illustrate the shaman as he presumed he looked while in the supernatural. This is clearly the case for the "patterned body anthropomorphs" — humans with elaborate internal body markings. These internal body markings were the shamans' "signs of power": geometric patterns that were believed to stand for his supernatural powers and spirits (see below). The shaman not only portrayed himself adorned with these geometric images, but he painted them on the ceremonial shirt which he wore during ceremonies. Though this ritual shirt is shown on many of these human petroglyph figures, these are not simply portrayals of shamans in the "real" world because they all lack human faces. Their geometrically-stylized faces are additional signs of power. The most common of these are concentric circles or spirals. These symbolized the whirlwind, which was believed to carry the shaman into the supernatural world and to concentrate power. The use of these motifs for the faces of the shamans was no accident. Like the whirlwind, the shaman was believed to concentrate supernatural power.

Some human figures are shown very small, grouped in lines. These are ceremonial dancers and they reflect the fact that the shaman was believed to "receive" all of his ceremonies and rituals while in his trance. They record a vision of a ceremony, which probably served to structure the way that a shaman conducted his rituals for the rest of his life.

Other humans are shown killing bighorns. For many years archaeologists believed these "hunter and sheep" motifs were evidence of a hunting cult in the Cosos, with the petroglyphs made for "hunting magic". Native Americans consistently denied the existence of any custom of this kind, and archaeological excavations have failed to uncover evidence of such a cult, or even evidence of significant sheep hunting in this region. More recently, detailed studies of Native American beliefs and symbols have allowed us to understand these "hunting scenes". They represent complex metaphors for the making of rain, based on the fact that the rain shaman was believed to change into a bighorn spirit when he went into the supernatural realm to make rain, and to "die" or "kill himself" when he went into a trance. This last belief is partly based on the physical and emotional similarities between death and entering a trance (falling over, diminished vital signs, convulsions, feelings of grief, etc.). Making rain required a kind of ritual auto-sacrifice on the part of the shaman, which is what these motifs portray.

▼ Geometric motifs are signs of power.

At many rock art sites geometric motifs of various kinds are the most common images. The Cosos are unusual in this respect because readily identifiable "iconic" or representational images of sheep, humans and other animals are so frequently seen. But even in the Cosos, geometric forms represent about one-quarter of the petroglyph total, and they too require explanation.

Certain earlier archaeologists thought that the difference between the geometric and iconic motifs reflected differences in age and the evolution, over time, of artistic abilities. It was believed that, in older times, people only had the ability to draw (and engrave) crude geometric images. The capability for iconic image-making developed later, as humans became "more advanced". From this perspective the conclusion is that geometric designs are necessarily older than iconic motifs. But we now know that this evolutionary hypothesis is wrong. Human artistic ability evolves over the lifetime of an individual (from child to adult), but did not evolve in this fashion during the long span of the human occupation of the world. Since our species first appeared, humans have always had the same artistic abilities that we have today.

To understand the meaning of the geometric motifs, archaeologists more recently have turned to studies of the neuropsychology of trance. They have found that, during hallucinatory experiences, a series of widely-shared kinds of mental images are generated within our mind. These are "pictures in the mind's eye", and they can occur during a trance regardless of culture, individual, or time period in question. This is because they are generated by our neuroanatomical system, which all humans share. One kind of mental image commonly occurring during a trance is a set of geometric light patterns known as entoptics ("within the eye"). Zigzags, spirals, dots, meanders, grids, parallel lines, and nested curves are the most common entoptic forms that our optical systems generate during a trance, but many others also can be "seen" in our mind, and they can combine and fragment in a seemingly endless number of ways. Entoptics may also appear during a migraine headache, or simply if you stare at a bright light and then rub your eyes.

The geometric petroglyphs can be understood as examples of these entoptic patterns generated during a shaman's trance. Because a shaman experienced these entoptic/geometric images along with iconic forms such as animal spirit helpers, it is clear that these two kinds of petroglyphs do not differ in age, and in fact were often made by the same artist.

This neuropsychological information tells us how these geometric motifs originated, but it does not explain what they symbolized. The meaning can only come from the accounts of Native Americans. For example, they have told us that concentrics and spirals symbolized the whirlwind, the concentrator of supernatural power, and that zigzags stood for rattlesnakes. The meaning of the numerous remaining entoptic forms and geometric motifs is unknown in any specific sense, although it is clear that, in a general way, they were intended to serve as signs of supernatural power.

▼ Petroglyphs are dated in three ways; some may be over 16,000 years old.

Petroglyphs are dated in three ways. First, items depicted in the art are sometimes specific to a particular time period, and thereby give us information about chronology. Horses were only introduced into the region during the last 200 years, for example, so depictions of horses and riders necessarily are less than a few hundred years in age. Archaeological research has shown that, about 1500 years ago, the bow and arrow were introduced into the region, quickly replacing the atlatl, or throwing board, and dart. Bow and arrow motifs, or humans holding bows, are then less than 1500 years old, while depictions of atlatls — often shown as a long, straight vertical line bisecting a small circle near its lower end — are greater than 1500 years in age. Motifs that are believed to portray large animals that went extinct during the Ice Age, more than 11,000 years ago, have been identified at a few other Mojave Desert sites. Although these identifications are tentative, they suggest great age for at least some of the petroglyphs.

A second way of determining age involves the examination of a motif's relative condition. Petroglyphs were made by pecking away the dark rock varnish coating to reveal the lighter heart rock below. This rock varnish (sometimes called, incorrectly, "patina") is made of very small particles of wind-borne dust that, over time, are cemented by microbes onto the rock surface. Once a petroglyph has been made, this varnishing process starts over again within the engraved-out lines or areas of the motif. All things being equal, we can compare the relative degree of revarnishing between two or more motifs to determine which is the oldest; this would be the motif that is darkest or most heavily revarnished.

This approach to dating is difficult because all things usually aren't equal, and varnish coatings will form at very different rates on different rock panels because of a variety of very local environmental conditions. As a result, it is very difficult to use differences in the relative degree of revarnishing as an indicator of age for motifs located on different rock panels. Still, systematic studies of the relative degree of revarnishing on a large number of Coso petroglyphs showed that all humans with bows and arrows had little or no visible evidence of revarnishing. Since these motifs are necessarily less than 1500 years old, a very general rule of thumb is that petroglyphs that look "fresh" were most likely made less than 1500 years ago.

Chronometric techniques have been developed and are now being used to date the Coso petroglyphs, the final way of determining their age. These are complicated chemical, morphological and nuclear analyses of the rock varnish coating the petroglyphs. They allow archaeologists to assign specific ages to individual motifs. Our chronometric petroglyph dates suggest that the first Coso petroglyphs were made over 16,000 years ago, and that they continued to be engraved into the last few hundred years.

This last inference is supported by the presence of an occasional historical horse and rider motif, as well as by the historical accounts of Native Americans. That Native Americans discussed and described the making and meaning of the petroglyphs is a clear indication that they were still making these motifs into the relatively recent past. To the best of our knowledge, the most recent examples of Coso rock art were made by shamans in the first few decades of the twentieth century.

While none of these dating techniques is perfect or even very exact, when viewed in combination they provide a fairly clear picture of the chronology of the Coso petroglyphs. Reasonable support exists for the belief that the first petroglyphs were made during the Ice Age, as much as 16,500 years ago. Petroglyph making appears to have been sporadic for much of the remainder of prehistory. It was only during the last 1000 to 2000 years that most of the petroglyphs in the Cosos (and other parts of the Mojave Desert) were created. While some of the Coso art is very ancient, the majority of the motifs that you will see are much younger and were engraved in the last 1000 or so years, with many of the petroglyphs probably being only a few hundred years old.

▼ HELP PRESERVE THE PETROGLYPHS

Little Petroglyph Canyon is truly a national treasure, and it is understandable that many people are interested in visiting it. But it is also true that we all need to make efforts to preserve and protect this treasure so that future generations can also enjoy this rock art. Ensuring that your visit is not detrimental to this art is relatively simple, and requires following a few obvious rules. Do not climb on or walk over the petroglyphs. Do not touch them with your fingers or hands. Do not "chalk them" or splash them with water to make them (momentarily) more visible. Do not take rubbings or make castings of them. Obviously, do not create graffiti or leave trash in the canyon. But, please, correct the improper behavior of other visitors that you may observe. Usually, improper behavior simply results from lack of information, and properly caring for the petroglyphs is everybody's business.

For thousands of years Little Petroglyph Canyon has been a sacred place to Native American peoples. If you remember this fact, and act as you would in our own culture's sacred places, this will do much to ensure that your visit is harmless to this important aspect of our cultural heritage.

II
TAKING THE WALKING TOUR

▼

The remainder of this guide is a walking tour in Little Petroglyph Canyon that you can follow from the parking lot at the top down to the end of the petroglyphs, which takes you generally in a southerly direction. Little Petroglyph Canyon (or Lower Renegade Canyon, as it is sometimes called) is a natural arroyo that cuts into Wild Horse Mesa, a rugged upland area of the Cosos. You will walk down the canyon bottom, which alternates between deep sandy washes, rocky cobbles, and water-smoothed bedrock. Far from an easy walk down a country lane, at times you may be slogging through the sand, clambering over rock outcrops, or hopping from cobble to cobble. This information is not intended to scare anyone away. In fact, many of the best panels are close to the parking area and can be visited by everyone, so Little Petroglyph Canyon can be enjoyed without an arduous hike. Moreover, this guide has been designed partly to emphasize the rock art towards the top end of the canyon, close to the parking lot, to ensure that all visitors have the opportunity to benefit from their experience in the canyon. But this guide will also allow those planning on the complete hike to learn as much as possible at the outset, so they will understand more about the petroglyphs as they move down canyon.

If you want to see all of the petroglyphs and all of the panels discussed in this guide, walking to the end of the canyon is required, and it is important to be prepared for your hike down the canyon in order to enjoy it to the fullest. Important things to take along are: hiking boots; plenty of water on your person (and in your car, so that you will have water to return to); a hat and/or sunshade; snacks or a lunch, if you plan to stay in the canyon for any length of time; and your camera, with plenty of film. In Little Petroglyph Canyon the general rule of thumb is to take twice as much film as you think you will need, and this may be enough. A walking stick is also useful to help with balance and to forewarn any dozing rattlesnakes. Weather is unpredictable in the Cosos during the fall and spring. Be prepared for hot and for cold and windy conditions.

The two biggest dangers in the canyon are twisted ankles, caused by slipping off rocks, and rattlesnakes, which nature provides free of charge. Both dangers are exacerbated by the fact that most visitors travel down canyon with their eyes firmly directed toward the canyon walls, to see the petroglyphs. Though understandable, this is dangerous. Pay attention to your path, and be very careful where you put your feet and hands. The rattlesnakes blend in very well with their surroundings.

One other caution is necessary. Little Petroglyph Canyon lies within an active missile test range. While the canyon itself has been excluded from the practice range for many years, it is possible that old unexploded ordnance might still be present. So do not pick up any metal objects in the canyon, and report any that you observe to your tour leader.

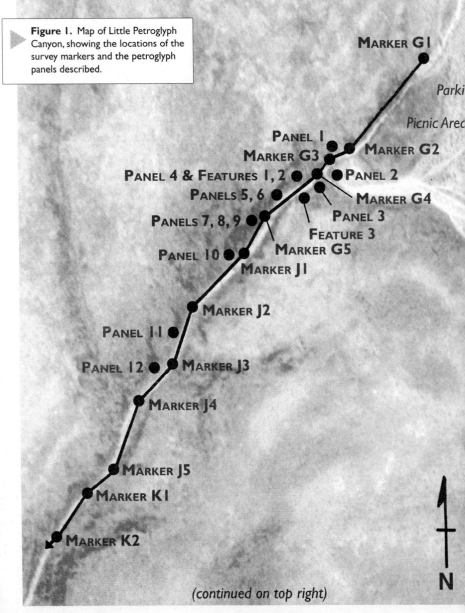

Figure 1. Map of Little Petroglyph Canyon, showing the locations of the survey markers and the petroglyph panels described.

MARKER G1

Parki

Picnic Area

PANEL 1
MARKER G3
MARKER G2
PANEL 4 & FEATURES 1, 2
PANEL 2
PANELS 5, 6
MARKER G4
PANELS 7, 8, 9
PANEL 3
FEATURE 3
PANEL 10
MARKER G5
MARKER J1
MARKER J2
PANEL 11
PANEL 12
MARKER J3
MARKER J4
MARKER J5
MARKER K1
MARKER K2

N

(continued on top right)

From the parking lot to the bottom of the canyon is a distance of about two kilometers (1.2 miles; Fig. 1). Given the terrain, this is about a 45 minute walk, one way, with no time for sightseeing. The walking tour down canyon is roughly a two hour trip, one-way, allowing time to examine, read about, and photograph the panels. (Obviously different people will progress down canyon at different speeds, so this is only a very general estimate). Remember that this is a one-way estimate. Make sure that you allow

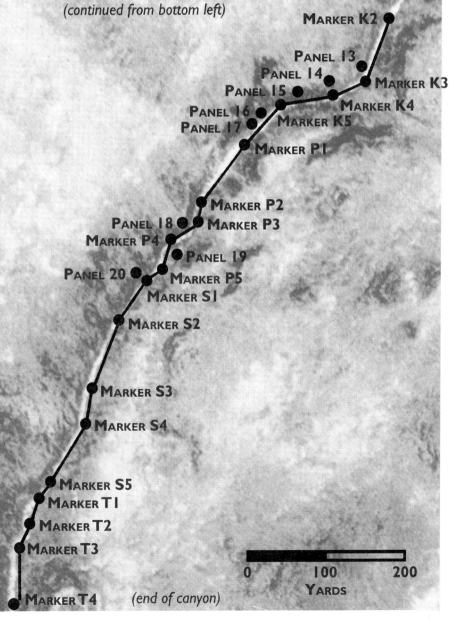

(continued from bottom left)

MARKER K2

PANEL 13
PANEL 14
PANEL 15
MARKER K3
MARKER K4
PANEL 16
MARKER K5
PANEL 17
MARKER P1

MARKER P2
PANEL 18
MARKER P3
MARKER P4
PANEL 19
PANEL 20
MARKER P5
MARKER S1
MARKER S2

MARKER S3

MARKER S4

MARKER S5
MARKER T1
MARKER T2
MARKER T3

0   100   200
YARDS

MARKER T4   (end of canyon)

sufficient time to get back to your car so that you are ready to depart on time with your tour group. Failure to do so may jeopardize the museum's ability to take future trips into the canyon!

▼ GETTING STARTED

The walking tour is keyed to a series of survey markers that have been placed in the bottom of the canyon, which you can use as reference points to locate the petroglyph panels that are described and discussed below. These markers are brass caps (Fig. 2), about three inches in diameter, that have been permanently fixed to rocks in or near the canyon bottoms. Each is identified with a unique stamped letter and number, such as "G1", "S2", etc. Watch for these as you move down canyon. They are sometimes hard to find, and occasionally may get covered with sand by a seasonal storm, but your vigilance in searching for them will make locating the petroglyph panels discussed in this guide easier, and it will also help you avoid rattlesnakes and twisted ankles. If you miss one of the markers you should be able to reestablish your position as you continue to move down canyon and encounter the next.

Please note that only certain rock art panels are discussed in this guide. Many, many more are not mentioned, simply because it would be an impossible task to cover all of the rock art in the canyon, as you will quickly realize. Those that are discussed are primarily included because they provide good examples illustrating what we know about the Coso petroglyphs. You are likely to find additional panels and motifs that you find particularly pleasing or interesting. The discussion presented below will help you understand your personal favorites too.

You will also note that most of the panels discussed will be on your right as you move down canyon. This is because the left side of the canyon faces northwest and tends to have a significant growth of lichens as a result. The lichens often obscure the petroglyphs on this side, making the southeastwards facing panels on your right easier to see and photograph.

▼ PARKING LOT TO CANYON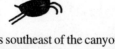

You will park your car in the designated lot that is southeast of the canyon, which has a series of outhouses. You may want to take advantage of these before you get underway, because there are no such facilities once you are in the canyon.

From the parking lot, walk down a well-trodden sandy path towards the west to approach the canyon. You will pass a fenced picnic area on your right hand side (fenced to keep out burros), and a field of small basalt cobbles. A short path then turns to your right, which will lead you down into the canyon. It is marked by a pole with flagging. As you take this short path toward the north, you will notice an upright boulder with petroglyphs and a brass plaque commemorating

3 DIMENSIONAL SURVEY CONTROL
CSU FRESNO
STATION
C3
YEAR
1992
SURVEYING ENGINEERING
DO NOT DISTURB

Figure 2. Survey markers used in the tour

the placement of Little Petroglyph Canyon on the National Register of Historic Places.

This rock art panel is a useful illustration of the variation in the relative degree of revarnishing that different petroglyphs exhibit. Many of the motifs on this boulder are darkly revarnished and, at least in very general terms, may be assumed to be relatively ancient. As you move into and then down the canyon the motifs typically are much more lightly revarnished, and therefore most likely younger. Some petroglyphs are near the canyon bottom and lack revarnishing entirely, but this fact is due to water scouring rather than relative youthfulness. Remember, then, that the rate of revarnishing in a particular motif depends on very localized conditions, so that comparisons between panels in different places are difficult to interpret. Still, the motifs on this particular boulder are among the most heavily revarnished in the canyon, and we can speculate that they may be among the oldest.

You will enter the canyon about 50 feet north (upstream) of Marker G3, which is in the middle of the canyon bottom. The designations on the markers increase as you move down canyon (G2, G3, G4, etc.). Try to locate the first survey marker as soon as you are in the canyon bottom, to facilitate keeping track of them as you proceed on the tour.

▼ Eastern end of the canyon

After finding your first survey marker, head upstream, which will take you north along the short upper reaches of the canyon. The canyon is shallow in this area and, relatively quickly, terminates on the flats of Wild Horse Mesa. The shallowness of the canyon here has an important effect on the petroglyphs. Many of them were necessarily engraved close to the canyon floor, on rocks that are seasonally scoured by flash floods. This prevents the development of rock varnish on the low-lying rocks and within the petroglyphs. In Little Petroglyph Canyon, the scoured and unvarnished basalt rocks are a characteristic light bluish-gray color.

Panel 1: Although you will immediately see many petroglyphs, the first panel to note is upstream (north) from Marker G3. It will be on your left side as you head up canyon, near the top of the canyon rim, on a panel that faces slightly downstream. It is a long "ladder-like" motif that stretches vertically from the bottom to the top of the panel (Fig. 3). This is a good example of an entoptic pattern. (It is doubtful that it is a ladder, because Native Americans in this region did not make two-pole ladders of this type). Entoptics are the geometric light images that are generated within the optical system during the hallucinations of a trance. Shamans made petroglyphs to depict the hallucinatory images they experienced during their vision quests, with entoptic patterns among the most common images they experienced, hence the commonness of the geometric petroglyphs here and at other rock art sites in the region. We do not know precisely what most of these entoptic patterns symbolized, which is not surprising since many of them are unique (and therefore idiosyncratic) images. But the historical Native American accounts indicate that, at a general level, they were "signs of power," representations of the fact that supernatural power — itself an abstract concept — had manifest itself to a shaman during his trance.

Although there is a recognized "set" of the most common entoptic patterns experienced during a trance, considerable variability actually occurs, which is amply illustrated by the myriad forms of geometric designs in the canyon. Another characteristic of the mental images seen during a trance is the combination of different images into a single "integrated" design, or the "juxtapositioning" of two abutting motifs. These characteristics are very evident in the canyon and, as you shall see, show up in the entoptic/geometric motifs as well as in the more recognizable iconic images.

You will also note many other motifs, geometric/entoptic and iconic, in this part of the canyon. One worth looking for is a large outline petroglyph of a bighorn sheep. This is very deeply engraved into the rock, but is located near the canyon bottom so that neither the panel nor the petroglyph itself have developed a rock varnish coating. This petroglyph will be on your right side as you move up canyon, above Marker G2.

> **Figure 3.** Ladder-like motif

▼ Near Marker G4

Once you have viewed the short northeastern end of the canyon, turn around and head back downstream. About 25 yards (approximately 25 paces) below Marker G3 (near where you first entered the canyon) you will encounter Marker G4. There are a number of things to see in this immediate area.

PANEL 2: To your left, as you face downstream, is a very short side canyon that joins with the main canyon at this point. On the right (western) side of this side canyon, near the juncture, is a panel showing two bowmen shooting at one another (Fig. 4)*. There are a number of interesting features to note here. The first is the weaponry: bows and arrows. Archaeological evidence has shown that bows first appeared in this region at about A.D. 500, and that they quickly replaced the older atlatl, or throwing board. Petroglyphs depicting bows must be less than 1500 years old, thereby giving us a rough estimate of the age of these petroglyphs. You will note that they are relatively "fresh" looking, and display little evidence of revarnishing.

A second attribute of these motifs is evident on the feet of the human on the right. Each has more than five toes. Hallucinations of extra digits are common during trance, which tells us something very important about this panel. It is not intended to portray a "real" event — a kind of prehistoric "shoot-out" between two bowmen — but instead depicts a supernatural occurrence, because it shows the hallucinatory effects of a trance.

What then does this panel symbolize? According to historical and modern Native American accounts, shamans sometimes induced trances to commit acts of sorcery, entering the sacred realm to use its power to bewitch an enemy. This was possible because supernatural power was amoral. It was intrinsically neither good nor bad but could be put to either purpose, depending on the intentions of an individual shaman. One result of this belief was a "malpractice" tradition with extreme consequences. A shaman that was hired to cure a sick individual was sometimes put to death if his cure was ineffective, because it was believed that he was using his supernatural power to bewitch rather than to heal his patient. (One very sad consequence of this belief was a rash of what the Euro-American authorities thought were Native American murders on Owens Valley reservations during the 1870s. Subsequently they recognized that these were deaths of shamans who were killed because of their understandable inability to cure a measles epidemic which ran through the region at that time).

Bewitching an individual was believed to involve projecting a "disease object," called "magical airshot," into the victim's bodies. (Curing rituals then often involved a sucking procedure in which the putative disease object was removed, and displayed, by the shaman). In many Native American languages, the same word was used for "arrow" and "magical airshot," because the disease object was a metaphorical arrow. A vision of shooting an arrow into another human, as shown in this panel, symbolizes a supernatural act of sorcery, the supernatural injection of the disease object into an opponent.

---

* In this photo and in the following petroglyph photos, the white bar is 10 cm long.

Figure 4. Two men shooting at one another

PANEL 3: A second interesting panel within this short side canyon is located at the far end of it, on the left side. This panel displays a series of rectangular "medicine bags" (Fig. 5). These are skin receptacles that were used to hold and carry the shaman's kit of ritual paraphernalia, the various ceremonial objects that he used in his ritual acts. Most commonly, medicine bags were made from badger or weasel skin. Many are shown with a horizontal stick across the top opening that served as a stretcher bar and handle, and some are shown fringed at the bottom.

The depiction of these "material culture artifacts" in the rock art raises an important point. The shaman was believed to see (and therefore receive) all of his supernatural power, his power songs and chants, his ceremonial practices, and his ritual items while in his trance. From our western perspective it is obvious that he did not "obtain" material artifacts like skin bags from the supernatural. What he "obtained" was the concept and idea for them, and he then made these ritual items later, after his vision. This explains why we see certain material artifacts in the art, as well as a specific range of such items. The depicted artifacts portray the kinds of implements used in rituals. As we shall see, this included weaponry, which played an important part in the Numic shaman's ceremonial kit, but it also excluded the vast majority of material culture artifacts such as huts, sandals, baskets, grinding stones and so on, that are not displayed in the art.

Figure 5. Medicine bags

▼ Marker G4 down canyon to G5

Return to Marker G4 in the main canyon. There is a dense concentration of petroglyphs and other features in this stretch of the canyon, so there is much to see right away.

PANEL 4: One of the first petroglyph panels you will notice is on your right as you face down the main canyon at Marker G4. This is located roughly at eye-level and vaguely resembles a "keyhole" on its side (Fig. 6). It consists of an outlined cross on the left abutting an oblong "cartouche" filled with "Xs" on the right. Another oblong/rectangle also filled with "Xs" is immediately below. These two geometric motifs are typical entoptic patterns, the light images created within the optical system during a trance. The upper petroglyph also illustrates the fact, noted above, that our mental images are often crowded together during hallucinations, sometimes running together, sometimes overlapping one another, and sometimes combining into very complex geometric patterns.

> **Figure 6.** "Keyhole" motif

Although we have little Native American information to guide our interpretation of most entoptic petroglyphs — reflecting the fact that most were probably idiosyncratic anyway — these two motifs are exceptions. Both of the oblong "cartouches" are filled with what are called "diamond-chains" (rows of connected "Xs"). Diamond-chains were universally used in Native California as a stylized representation of the diamondback rattlesnake because this geometric pattern resembles the scale pattern on the snake's back. (Zigzags also symbolized rattlesnakes because they mimic the track of a sidewinder in the sand). These two petroglyphs, then, are stylized representations of rattlesnakes.

Rattlesnake-shamans were said to receive their special supernatural powers from visions of snakes. These powers included the ability to cure snake bites, to handle rattlesnakes without threat of harm, and to transform into snake spirits while in the supernatural. Although all shamans could cure in general terms, rattlesnake power and therefore the ability to cure snake bites was one of the most common of the specialized kinds of potency that shamans could obtain during their visions.

That these two motifs may be recognized both as entoptic patterns and as identifiable stylizations of rattlesnakes raises an important point. The perception of entoptic patterns is potentially universal to all humans, because entoptics are generated within our shared optical systems. But how entoptic patterns were interpreted is obviously specific to the culture in question. Zigzags were interpreted as rattlesnakes in Native California and the Great Basin, following commonly shared cultural guidelines. On the Plains, in contrast, zigzags were interpreted as lightning and were symbolically related to the concept of the thunderbird. Symbolic meaning varied between different cultures and regions.

There was a strong tendency for cultures to apply specific symbolic meaning to the most common entoptic forms and for individuals to attempt to "decipher" or "interpret" the entoptic patterns that occurred during visions in terms of culturally meaningful symbols and iconic images. We call this tendency "construal," and it is a common characteristic of the hallucinations of trance. Our minds will always attempt to understand what they are seeing and, if they can't, they will project a "closest fit" interpretation onto the image in our head. This is why we often "see" things that aren't really there when it is dark. Our visual imagery is impaired by the darkness, but our mind will still attempt to generate a meaningful pattern out of the partial images that we are seeing.

Many of the identifiable iconic or representational petroglyphs, including some of the bighorn sheep as well as these rattlesnake motifs, thus had their origin in entoptic patterns that were interpreted or construed by the shaman as a culturally meaningful image. As we shall see, this accounts for the "stylization" of many of the identifiable petroglyphs.

FEATURE 1: There is another feature just beyond this panel (and on the same side) that is worth noting. This is a horizontal boulder face that has a circular, ground smooth area, immediately adjacent to an entoptic/geometric petroglyph (Fig. 7). "Grinding slicks", or bedrock metates as these are called, were used to grind seeds into meal using a handstone or mano. The juxtaposition of the petroglyph with the seed grinding surface has caused some archaeologists to infer either that the petroglyphs were not made in rituals, or that the ritual

Figure 7. Grinding slick

necessarily was related to plant food gathering and processing. The basis for this inference is the commonly held archaeological belief that if two things are found together they must have been used together. And since we know that grinding slicks were used to process seeds, the petroglyphs must have been tied somehow to this subsistence activity. The deeper (and rarely recognized) archaeological assumption underlying these kinds of inferences is the related notion that all cultures separate their sacred and religious ceremonies from their mundane activities.

Although our own western culture tends to restrict its religious activities to specific sacred places — our churches and cemeteries — Native American cultures made no such distinction, reflecting their belief that the quality of sacredness is present everywhere, to some degree. Their distinction between sacred and non-sacred was more a question of time rather than place. We find their deceased buried in the middle of village sites. We know that, at particular times, ceremonial dances and rituals were also conducted in the middle of villages and, in some cases, rock art was also made within a village. In each case this does not imply an absence of sacredness or connection with ritual, but instead the fact that sacred activities were as much tied to particular times — ritual periods — as to specific locations. While Little Petroglyph Canyon clearly was a sacred place, it was also used at certain times for mundane activities. Grinding seeds on this bedrock metate was one of those mundane activities.

FEATURE 2: If you walk a few steps beyond this grinding slick you will notice a series of shallow ground depressions in the rocks on both sides of the canyon (Fig. 8). These are called "cupules". That they were placed on a variety of rock surfaces, including vertical faces, is a clear indication that they did not serve a "practical function," like grinding seeds. Although not rock art in the sense used here, cupules were made during rituals, and they reflect some of the same general symbolism and beliefs as the petroglyphs, even though they weren't made by shamans and do not depict visionary images. In this portion of California, cupules were made by young girls during puberty rituals that signaled the arrival of womanhood. As such, the cupules had a variety of levels of symbolic meaning. The most obvious of these concerns the woman's traditional role in Native American society as the gatherer and preparer of plant foods, an activity that sometimes involved the use of bedrock mortars and pestles. At the superficial level, the making of the cupules ritually duplicated the use of the mortar and pestle, thereby ceremonially emphasizing the role the young woman was about to assume in her society.

Probably more important were the deeper levels of symbolic meaning attached to this girls' ritual. One of these concerns beliefs about the rocks found at rock art sites. These were thought to serve as the boundary between the supernatural and natural worlds. Spirits were said to reside within the rocks and, when shamans went into the supernatural realm, cracks in the rock face were believed to open up so that the shaman could enter the sacred region. By grinding into the rock surface, the girls were accessing the supernatural realm. Then, taking some of the rock powder and putting it on themselves, they were anointed with a small measure of supernatural power which helped to insure their health and success later in life. This was one of the primary purposes of the puberty initiation.

A third level of meaning involves the sexual symbolism implicit in using a phallus-like pestle to grind a vagina-like depression in a rock. (In certain ceremonies, Native Americans used pestles that were shaped like immense phalluses, demonstrating that this sexual symbolism was widely recognized.) The making of the cupules was, in this sense, a symbolic act of ritual intercourse, showing that the young girls had reached the age of menarche and were ready for marriage and procreation. Procreation was more than simply a physical act for, as the ceremony suggested, it required supernatural power to occur.

The fact that the cupules had various levels of meaning is neither unique nor even unusual. All symbols have multiple levels of meaning, including the petroglyphs in the canyon. At a superficial level, their presence marked this canyon as a location where supernatural power reached close to the surface of the earth. At another level, each petroglyph signaled that a particular individual had become a shaman or "man of power" at that specific spot. And, at a third level, they symbolized the nature of the supernatural events he had experienced and the kinds of power he obtained and used.

The localization of the grinding slicks and cupules in this portion of the

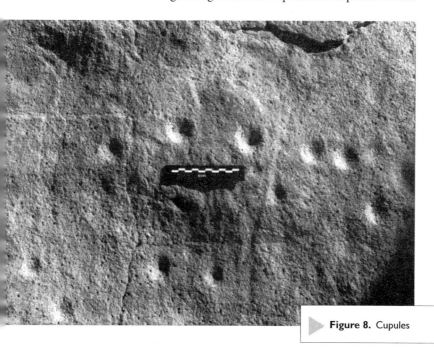

Figure 8. Cupules

canyon is no accident. A small prehistoric camp site is located nearby, with these non-shamanic features concentrated close to the living area.

As you move deeper into the canyon you will discover that such features become less common the further you travel from this camp.

PANEL 5: A short distance down canyon you will notice a boulder on your right, at the base of the canyon wall, with a seemingly random line engraved along the edge of the rock (Fig. 9). This is a fairly common occurrence in the petroglyphs; aspects of the rock surface are used in the composition of the motif. This petroglyph is a simple example of this phenomenon, with more elaborate ones including figures of humans shown as if they are emerging out of cracks in the rock. Regardless of the specific case, the use of the rock as a part of the motif occurs because a shaman would sometimes stare at the rock face during his trance. The rock surface would then serve as the external visual input for the mental images of the shaman's hallucinations and would influence the generation of the entoptic patterns within his optical system, including the form of any iconic image he might "see" or imagine he was seeing.

Shamans believed that spirits lived in the supernatural world which lies inside the rocks. The rocks were then permeable barriers that could be crossed by spirits and by humans with supernatural power, as they moved back and forth from the supernatural to the natural world. Sometimes the shaman saw a spirit that he believed was present in the supernatural realm during his trance. As he stared into the rock and hallucinated, a visual pattern began to appear in his mind,

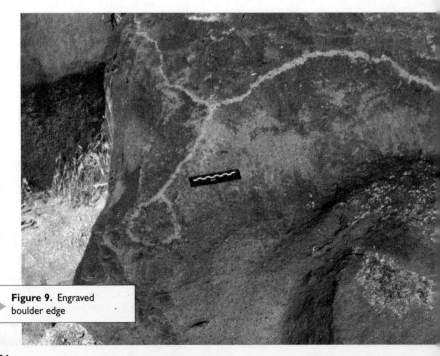

Figure 9. Engraved boulder edge

which was taken to mean that the spirit was emerging out of the supernatural world that lay on the other side of the rock face.

FEATURE 3: Continuing a short distance down the canyon toward Marker G5, an important archaeological feature is located on your left, up against the canyon wall. This is a pile of boulders and rocks that includes a large flat slab that has fallen against another boulder, creating a small low rockshelter (Fig. 10). This is a vision quest structure, a small temporary refuge that was used while the

Figure 10. Vision quest structure

shaman sat, sometimes for days, fasting, perhaps smoking tobacco, and waiting for his vision to appear. Although this pile of rocks is largely natural, some of the rocks have been purposely piled into a low stone wall, demonstrating its intentional human construction and prehistoric use. Please be very careful when viewing this feature. Do not remove or disturb any of the rocks, and do not attempt to climb into the overhang. Doing so will destroy this fragile feature, and will prevent future generations from appreciating this interesting aspect of Little Petroglyph Canyon.

Rock features such as this are fairly common in the Cosos. They include low walls and stone "circles" within rockshelters, as well as pit-like depressions in rocky talus slopes. For many years archaeologists interpreted these features as "hunting blinds." Because they are often found near rock art sites, this was taken as further evidence (beyond the depictions of animals in the art) that the rock art was made for purposes of hunting magic. Unfortunately, no one ever bothered to consider whether these so-called hunting blinds were satisfactorily placed for purposes of hunting. A knowledgeable hunter would obviously place his blind in a high position where game is unlikely to see him, with an unimpeded view of the surrounding terrain. As is immediately obvious, this rock feature and other similar ones are truly "blind," yielding a very poor view of the canyon, and thus being unusable for hunting. This rock feature also lacks any evidence of hunting weaponry or butchery, which we would expect to find at a hunting blind. Instead, it provides archaeological confirmation of the historical Native American accounts that tell us that petroglyphs resulted from the shaman's vision quest.

▼ MARKER G5 TO J1

Marker G5 is about 95 yards below G4. A number of important panels are located near Marker G5, including the most famous petroglyph from the Cosos.

PANEL 6: The first important panel in the Marker G5 vicinity is located a little up canyon from the marker (slightly behind you as you stand at the marker facing down canyon) and up high, on the right side, near the top of the canyon wall. This panel has a large bleached-out area towards the bottom but from about midway up you will observe a series of long vertical lines, some with hooks on the upper end, bisecting circles (Fig. 11). These have been widely interpreted as stylized atlatls, which are throwing boards that were used to propel darts or short spears. The spears rested against the hooks at the top. Finger-holds were placed at the lower end. The bisected circles are believed to be exaggerated weights that increased the throwing force of the weapon.

Atlatls were used prehistorically until AD 500, when they were quickly replaced by the bow and arrow. This means that these atlatl motifs are more than 1500 years old. They are a good example of the fact that certain motifs can be dated, at least in a general sense.

Atlatl and bow and arrow motifs were part of the evidence cited by early archaeologists in support of the notion that the petroglyphs were made for hunting magic. Actually, only a small percentage of the motifs are weapons and, since Native Americans denied such practices, hunting magic seems an unlikely even if superficially appealing cause for the art. On the other hand, the Native American accounts indicate that during the historical period a special kind of Arrow-wound shaman existed. He had special warfare or fighting powers including the ability to heal arrow wounds and was supposedly impervious to arrows shot at him. Arrow-wound shamans also served as leaders for wars and raids. During historical times these Arrow-wound shamans evolved into Gunshot-wound shamans with the same general kind of powers. (Although popularly associated with the Sioux, the Ghost Dance movement of the late nineteenth century actually originated with a Northern Paiute shaman, and incorporated many of these beliefs. It was believed that if believers wore special Ghost Dance shirts they would be impervious

Figure 11. Atlatls

to the bullets of the U.S. Cavalry.) Visions of weaponry and fighting were said to impart this specialized kind of supernatural power for both Arrow-wound and Gunshot-wound shamans, and bows and arrows were common ritual objects used by these shamans in their various ceremonies.

The antiquity of these atlatl motifs precludes the direct use of the historical Native American accounts for their interpretation. Still, it seems very likely that the Arrow-wound shamans evolved out of earlier Atlatl-wound shamans. We can speculate that the making of atlatl motifs was tied to similar beliefs and practices about visions of weaponry and violence.

PANEL 7: As you move down the canyon from Marker G5, watch for other depictions of atlatls on your right. These will be at mid-elevation, on a panel that shows one well-engraved atlatl, two rectangular "cartouches" and a series of fainter motifs (Fig. 12). The rectangular cartouches enclose geometric designs that are similar to those found within many of the elaborate human figures (see next panel below), and may represent "short-hand" or abbreviated renderings of these human figures. This speculation notwithstanding, it is clear that these cartouches encase entoptic patterns, the geometric designs generated in the optical system during a trance. The Native American accounts also indicate that these same entoptic designs were used by a shaman on many of his ritual objects. Though they were intended to portray his supernatural power, because each design was unique they came to serve as a kind of "signature piece" for the shaman.

PANEL 8: As you move further down the canyon roughly 30 to 40 yards beyond Marker G5, watch for a high panel, facing down canyon, that includes the frequently copied Coso Rain-shaman (Fig. 13). This panel contains four elaborate human figures, sometimes referred to as "patterned body anthropomorphs". Native American accounts indicate that figures such as these portray the shaman transformed into a spirit being. Like all such figures, they thereby combine natural and supernatural characteristics.

The famous large central figure contains features that provide specific clues to its symbolic meaning. The most important of these is the internal geometric design on the body. As noted above, this is an integration of the geometric/entoptic design that a shaman "saw" during his trance, and subsequently used to adorn his ritual robe and other paraphernalia. The "robe" was essentially a sack-like shirt or gown made of animal skin, sewn up on the sides, with sacred images painted on the front.

How do we know that these motifs aren't intended simply to depict the shaman in his natural state? That this is a supernatural spirit rather than natural being is indicated by the unnatural characteristics of the figure, most notably the head and face. All of the elaborate Coso human figures lack real faces, which have been replaced by some very stylized or geometric pattern. In this case it is a set of concentric circles. Concentrics and spirals symbolized the whirlwind.

Figure 12. Atlatl, two rectangular cartouches, etc.

Figure 13. Rain shaman

Whirlwinds were believed to contain spirits, to carry the shaman up into the supernatural world and, therefore, to be concentrators of supernatural power. With his face portrayed as a whirlwind, the shaman was also a concentrator of supernatural power. And, like the whirlwind, he had the supernatural power to fly.

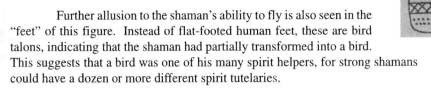

Further allusion to the shaman's ability to fly is also seen in the "feet" of this figure. Instead of flat-footed human feet, these are bird talons, indicating that the shaman had partially transformed into a bird. This suggests that a bird was one of his many spirit helpers, for strong shamans could have a dozen or more different spirit tutelaries.

The shaman's connection with bird spirits is further indicated by his headdress. Though described as "medusa-like" by some, it actually depicts a cap covered with the topknot feathers of the quail. The Rain-shaman in this region had a special ritual headdress — a cap made of bighorn sheep hide that had quail topknot feathers sewn on it. This particular shaman, like many who came to the Coso Range, thus had acquired the power to make rain, and hence the description of this motif as the Coso Rain-shaman.

Other notable aspects of this petroglyph are the objects in the shaman's hands: a curved stick in his right hand and three shorter straight sticks in his left. This combination and arrangement are fairly common for the elaborate human figures in this region. It is uncertain what these implements represent, although a bow and three arrows seems likely, suggesting that this figure is less than 1500 years old. Assuming that this interpretation is correct, it further emphasizes the ritual importance of weaponry in this art, as well as the relative youthfulness of many of these motifs.

PANEL 9: Another panel showing two elaborate human figures and additional motifs is located slightly further down the canyon, on your right, near the top of the canyon wall (Fig. 14). The larger of the two human figures, on the right side of the panel, has a checker-board-like pattern on its ritual shirt portraying the entoptic designs used by shamans as their signs of power. Note also the head, which again is a set of concentric circles, symbolizing the whirlwind. But, because of space problems on the panel, the head has been reduced and moved to the shoulder. This alteration further emphasizes that the importance of these motifs was not in faithful depiction of shamans in their natural state, but in defining characteristics as supernatural spirits in the sacred realm.

Both figures again have bird-talon feet, as is common with many of the Coso elaborate human figures. These talon-feet demonstrate the close association of shamans with birds, their perceived ability to fly using supernatural power, and the related fact that they had a bird of some kind as one of their spirit helpers.

The human figure on the left has a series of vertical zigzags on his ritual shirt. As noted previously, zigzags symbolized the sidewinder and probably indicate that this was a Rattlesnake-shaman, a shaman with the power to handle snakes, cure their bites, and transform into a snake spirit while in the supernatural realm.

▼ MARKER J1 TO J2

Marker J1 is about 70 yards below G5. Although the petroglyphs thin-

Figure 14. 2 shamans with checkerboard body & displaced concentric face

out for a distance between J1 and J2, there are some interesting panels in this portion of the canyon.

PANEL 10: Immediately below Marker J1 there is an important panel on your right that is near the top of the canyon wall and faces down canyon. This is a "scene" of three bighorn sheep, a stick-figure human, and an integration of geometric designs (Fig. 15). By know, you will have seen a number of bighorn sheep petroglyphs. They are overwhelmingly the most important animal motifs in the Cosos. While there are probably some local exceptions, bighorns tend to be the most common animal figures in the rock art of the western U.S. as a whole. Obviously bighorns were very important to Native Americans, and they therefore warrant some discussion.

Figure 15. "Rain scene" with hunter

Early archaeologists thought that the presence of presumed game animals in rock art indicated that the art was made for hunting magic. Native Americans disclaimed practicing any such ritual. Still, archaeologists persisted in this belief, assuming that the art could only pertain to what these people ate and denying that Native Americans had any kind of deeper religious beliefs and symbolism. But, recent attention to Shoshone and Paiute accounts has shown that the bighorn was the special spirit helper of the Rain-shaman, and that the Cosos were believed to be a place to which shamans could come from all over the Great Basin to acquire this specialized kind of power. The majority of the bighorn sheep petroglyphs depict the spirit helpers of the Rain-shamans.

Why the bighorn was symbolically associated with rain is not yet fully clear. Our current hypothesis is that Native Americans linked the bighorn with rain because bighorns descend from the mountain heights when (or immediately before) it starts raining, in order to browse on the fast-sprouting desert plants that result. The appearance of the bighorn then signals the appearance of rain. Although this interpretation is still speculative, what we know for certain is that the bighorn sheep and in some cases bighorn sheep rock art were widely associated with rain and stormy weather by Native Americans in the west.

This leads to the human figure on this panel, shown impaling a bighorn with a spear. If the petroglyphs weren't made for hunting magic, why do they sometimes show humans in the act of killing sheep? Correctly interpreting this symbolic imagery — a human killing a sheep — requires understanding Native American symbolism at a deep rather than superficial level, for this "hunter and sheep" imagery encodes many of the most important beliefs about and attributes of the shaman's vision quest.

The first of these is the fact that the shaman and his spirit helper were so intimately associated that there was no way to distinguish between the actions of a shaman and his spirit helper. The shaman became his spirit helper when he entered the supernatural realm. This fact caused much of the confusion among early archaeologists about the relationship of the rock art to historical Native Americans. When anthropologists asked Native Americans who had made the rock art, a common reply was that they had been made by spirits. Archaeologists assumed that this reflected a lack of knowledge on the part of the Native Americans, equating their statement about spirits with our beliefs about fairies and wood sprites. But in fact the anthropologists unknowingly had actually asked a question that touched on a common Native American taboo: speaking the name of a deceased individual, in this case a dead shaman. Native American informants answered this question in a way that avoided this taboo and that was perfectly understandable from their perspective. To them, rock art that was made by a spirit was obviously art that was created by a shaman. The two were indistinguishable and answering with a generic response ("spirits made the petroglyphs") avoided the dangers of naming a deceased shaman. It was the archaeologists, not the Native Americans, who were confused about this art and the Native Americans' relationship to it.

The second belief follows from the first. The depiction of a "human shooting a sheep" is not a depiction of a "real" event but is a portrayal of a bighorn shaman killing himself in his supernatural form. Understanding this symbolic concept requires recognizing that it is a graphic metaphor. Metaphors were used by Native Americans to describe supernatural experiences because hallucinations are essentially indescribable experiences. (Our culture also uses a series of slang metaphors to describe drug-induced hallucinations, such as "going on a trip," "being stoned," "spaced-out," etc., for the same reason. It is very difficult to describe hallucinatory experiences.) We have been able to decipher this graphic metaphor because it was also used verbally, and was recorded in some of the early Native American accounts. The metaphor used here, death or killing, is the single most common metaphor used to describe the visionary experience. Odd as this may seem at first, death or killing is an appropriate metaphor for entering the supernatural state for a couple of reasons. The first is the strong physical similarity between mortal death and a trance. In either case an individual will fall-over, vital signs will diminish, eyes may roll back, and convulsions may occur. A person in a trance is "lost to the world" and will appear as if dead. Second, trances often yield very strong emotional reactions. We commonly equate trance and visionary experiences with ecstatic or euphoric emotions, but these are not the only emotional reactions that may result. As law enforcement personnel know only too well, hallucinatory experiences can also lead to violent and/or grievous emotional reactions. In fact, laboratory experiments involving the administration of hallucinatory drugs to college students indicate that about 20% of the students report feeling the extreme emotional grief of seeing their own deaths.

The shaman's entry into the supernatural realm to make rain was not necessarily an ecstatic experience. In some cases it could be quite unpleasant, involving feeling his own death. This possibility caused the shaman's supernatural experience to be viewed as a kind of ritual auto-sacrifice. He "killed" himself to enter the supernatural realm, as these petroglyphs show. As is thus quite clear, the Coso petroglyphs encode much more than child-like images. They reflect a very complex mental and symbolic system. The mental world of our Native American forebears was as rich as our own, even if their lives were simpler than ours from the perspective of material wealth and its encumbrances.

As you move down the canyon from this panel, the canyon walls will be replaced by a hillside of smaller volcanic cobbles. These contain no petroglyphs, for obvious reasons. Just beyond this slope of cobbles is a good panel of atlatls located high on your right side, facing down canyon.

▼ MARKER J2 TO J3

The distance from Marker J1 to J2 is about 110 yards. As you move down the canyon below J2, the density of petroglyphs will start to increase. A very important panel is located about 25 yards below J2.

PANEL 11: This panel is located on the floor of the wash, on your right side, and partly faces down canyon. It contains a series of small bighorn petroglyphs, the most interesting of which are two outlined sheep shown with internal geometric body designs (Fig. 16). These are equivalent to the so-called "patterned body anthropomorphs" or elaborate human figures that have been described earlier (see Panels 8 and 9.) Just as shaman figures are shown incorporating their entoptic signs of power within their bodies, some bighorns have these same internal markings, thereby establishing an equivalence between sheep and humans. This illustration further emphasizes the fact that the sheep petroglyphs are not intended to portray real sheep but instead are sheep spirits, the supernatural helpers of the Rain-shamans. Other "patterned-body sheep" as

Figure 16. Patterned body sheep

well as biologically impossible bighorns (e.g., bighorns with two heads or three sets of horns) are fairly common in the canyon.

▼ MARKER J3 TO J4

An interesting concentration of petroglyphs is located below Marker J3.

These are in a small "alcove" or bowl created by a very small side canyon, roughly 10 yards long, entering the main canyon from your right. A number of panels are worth inspecting here.

PANEL 12: At the top of this alcove is a panel with a large bear paw print on its side, a crude bighorn, and some stylized atlatls (Fig. 17). The bear paw is particularly worth noting. Bears, especially grizzlies, were important

Figure 17. Large bearpaw print

animals for Native American shamans because they were dangerous. Supernatural power was considered intrinsically perilous. The degree of danger posed by a particular animal species was taken as a sign of that species' inherent supernatural power, with the most dangerous species most strongly linked to the shaman. (It is partly for this reason that animals such as rabbits were rarely if ever associated with shamans.) Grizzly bears and rattlesnakes were the most dangerous species in Native California, and they were very strongly associated with shamans as potential spirit helpers.

The use of a paw print to symbolize the grizzly spirit reflects a common characteristic of hunter-gatherer societies. The men were hunters and were accustomed to following animal tracks. Prints and tracks were then logical images used to portray animals as a whole, because they were so readily identifiable by all members of society.

One attribute of this bear paw is particularly worth noting. It has seven digits, illustrating the "polydactylism" — perception of extra digits during a trance — noted previously concerning Panel 2. This is not a portrayal of a natural bear but the supernatural spirit of a bear, probably received as a spirit helper by a shaman.

There are a series of other interesting panels within this alcove, including a cluster of small atlatls immediately above the bear paw. A lower panel (to your left as you face the bear paw) contains two very heavily revarnished zigzag-rattlesnake motifs, while some interesting human figures are located near the alcove's southern side.

▼ Marker J4 to J5, J5 to K1 & on to K2

It is about 100 yards from Marker J4 to J5, and then about 50 yards to K1 and another 75 yards to K2. Marker J5 is difficult to find. It is located on the left side of the canyon on top of some waterworn rocks, about three feet above the canyon floor, and across from a cobble scree slope. The density of petroglyphs is variable in this stretch, because of changing conditions of the rocks. The prehistoric shamans almost exclusively selected homogeneous faces of basalt bedrock or large boulders, and ignored the vesicular basalt and smaller cobbles.

Just before reaching Marker K1 you may notice a very crowded panel of petroglyphs on your left, including a number of bighorns, entoptics and miscellaneous motifs. Many of these appear to have been made by the same shaman-artist, judging from their revarnishing. This panel shows that the mental imagery generated by hallucinations is often not a neat composition of intentionally well-spaced images or designs. Instead, it may include images superimposed one upon another, butting together, inverted from a normal horizontal perspective, and so on. Characteristics of petroglyphs such as these do not prove that the motifs derive from efforts to portray the mental images of shamans' trances. But, these characteristics cannot be readily explained by any other hypothesis. They thus serve as important independent evidence in support of this interpretation of the art, which is otherwise primarily provided by the Native American accounts.

Another panel that you may notice in this same area is a relatively faint grouping of two bighorn sheep, one of which is "patterned-bodied", along with another four-legged animal, which is long-bodied, short-legged, with a long straight tail and no horns or antlers. Based on the tail posture this can be identified as a canid: a dog or coyote. (Mountain lions, in contrast, are shown with their tails curling forward to parallel their back, which is a tail posture that most dogs cannot easily assume.) Native American accounts indicate that visions of coyotes were portents of sorcery, and shamans sent coyote spirits to bewitch their enemies. Scenes such as this most likely represent supernatural efforts by a sorcerer to bewitch a bighorn spirit, or Rain-shaman. This is a reasonable interpretation since one of these bighorns is patterned-bodied, and thus obviously does not depict a natural sheep.

▼ MARKER K2 TO K3

The distance from Marker K2 to K3 is about 100 yards. Another important panel is located just before Marker K3.

PANEL 13: This is located on the right side of the canyon on a rock face that is almost horizontal and that faces down canyon. The canyon wall is very low in this area and this panel is close to the wash bottom.

Figure 18. Double-headed bighorn

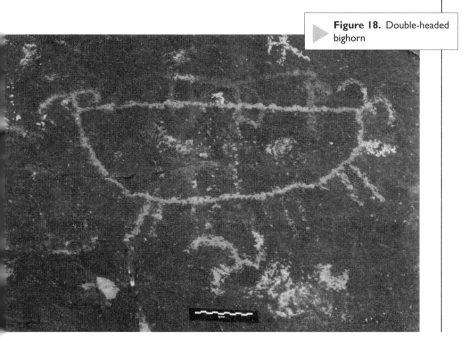

The panel contains a large outlined bighorn and a variety of other motifs (Fig. 18). The bighorn is notable because it is double-headed — a classic "push-me, pull-you" creature. As should now be clear, the Coso shamans were not attempting to portray natural bighorns that hunters might hope to encounter and kill during their hunts, but spirit beings, the animals of the supernatural world that the shaman saw during his trance.

▼ MARKER K3 TO K4

The distance between these survey markers is about 50 yards. As you move down this stretch of the canyon it starts to descend, with a large drop at Marker K4, the location of a large bedrock "waterfall." Your first drop will be at a much smaller bedrock waterfall roughly midway between the two markers. (There will be no water in either of these falls during your visit, except perhaps remnant pools at their bases, but you will see how the seasonal flash floods have scoured the basalt bedrock in these areas.) Just below the small waterfall is an attractive panel on your right that includes a series of bighorn sheep, a medicine bag, and a circle filled with dots. This panel is another example of the mixture of entoptic and iconic forms that appears during a shaman's trance. These different kinds of motifs are not different art "styles" from different time periods, or even from different artists, but may be part of the hallucinatory imagery of a single shaman's trance.

Although you should be careful during your entire trip, please look closely for rattlesnakes between Markers K3, K4 and K5. This seems to be the stretch of the canyon where they are most commonly seen.

▼ MARKER K4 TO K5

Marker K4 is at the top of a steep waterfall. It is a scramble to get down (and back up) this fall area but, if you are at all agile on rocks, it is worth the effort. The area below the waterfall contains one of the densest concentrations of petroglyphs in the Cosos.

PANEL 14: Before clambering down the falls, be sure to examine the large, almost horizontal, panel that is on the north side of the canyon (to your right as you face downstream), across from Marker K4. This panel contains two well-rendered medicine bags, a series of human figures and various entoptic/geometric forms (Fig. 19). One of the latter is a sinuous snake, further attesting to the importance of Rattlesnake-shamans in the region.

If you compare the patterned-body human figures on this panel with the others seen so far in the canyon (Panels 8 and 9, Figs. 13 and 14) again you will notice the absence of repetition in the designs shown on their ritual shirts. The absence of repetition is unlikely to have been an accident, and it seems probable

Figure 19. Patterned body humans, medicine bags, etc.

that prospective shamans studied the existing petroglyphs to come up with their own special designs. This uniqueness would suggest that not all of these geometric motifs were true spontaneously-generated entoptics, but that many were intentional compositions, each created as a unique "signature piece."

Having a unique design for each shaman might seem to contradict the idea that the motifs were all derived from trance imagery. However a key attribute of shamans was that they were conjurers who regularly practiced sleight-of-hand tricks to convince the common folk that they possessed supernatural power. In a shaman's "sucking cure," for example, he would secret some small object in his mouth so that he could produce it at the proper moment, claiming that it was the "disease object" injected through sorcery into the sick person by an evil shaman. Similarly, he might swallow a long strand of rawhide, wedging an end of it in his teeth. Then, at the proper moment during a ritual, he would pull out or regurgitate up the rawhide strip, which would now be swollen, giving the impression that the shaman was capable of regurgitating his intestines, and yet could continue to live. It is not surprising that some of the putative visionary imagery was perhaps less than completely so. But what is more important is that it was believed to be such, and that it represented the entoptic patterns of trance, even if this was only partly true.

Below the falls, you will travel through a stretch of very narrow, high-walled canyon, much of which is heavily scoured by seasonal storms. Some faint pictographs are present on both sides of the canyon near or at the end of the narrow rock chute. There is a red and white panel on the underside of a horizontal overhang on your right, and a red motif (perhaps a human figure; it is hard to make out) on your left. Just where the canyon opens up, there is also a series of black painted bighorns on your left, about ten feet overhead, including another "patterned-body sheep" on a panel that faces down-canyon. Currently we have no information about any difference between pictographs and petroglyphs relative to their meaning or age, or who made them. The fact that pictographs are located in the same places as petroglyphs and include the same kinds of motifs suggests that there may have been no real difference in the symbolism, origins, or meanings of these two kinds of rock art.

▼ Marker K5 to P1, P2 & P3

Once you are in the area where the canyon opens up again, you will quickly encounter Marker K5, which is about 75 yards from K4 (at the falls). This is an area of high canyon walls that extend from the end of the rock chute to an old wire fence to the south. These walls are covered with petroglyphs, extending from the bottom of the canyon up two or three stories to the canyon wall tops, creating a gallery of motifs. You will see numerous atlatls, including one that is very realistically rendered, myriad forms of bighorn sheep, including additional patterned-body sheep and sheep with as many as eight legs, entoptic patterns of seemingly endless form, and many human figures. Though it is difficult to select the most important or interesting panels from this vast array, a few of the more notable ones include the following:

Panel 15: Immediately before Marker K5 on your right side down low near the canyon floor is a dense array of dots (Fig. 20). Dot patterns are very typical entoptic designs, and are to be expected in rock art depicting trance imagery.

Nevertheless, there is no end of "explanations" that have been offered for rock art arrays of dots and their linear equivalents, tick marks. These

Figure 20. Dot pattern

range from calendrical counts of different kinds, to records of animal kills, to menstrual cycles, and so on. The problem is that there are any number of different "counting interpretations" possible for numbers of things, with little evidence to test these ideas. Barring directly relevant Native American accounts, these interpretations appear to be more a sign of the interests of the interpreter than of the creator of the rock art.

In the Coso case, we have no Native American accounts to explain repeated numbers of dots or ticks. Our closest accounts of such phenomena were obtained from Native American groups on the Columbia Plateau, commenting on tick marks. Columbia Plateau shamans, like those in the Coso region, also made rock art to portray their visionary imagery, indicating that this general cultural tradition was widespread across far western North America. The Columbia Plateau shamans' beliefs, thus, may also apply to the Cosos. The two different comments about Columbia Plateau tick marks are that: (1) they depict the number of days a shaman stayed on his vision quest; and (2) they portray the number of spirit helpers possessed by a shaman.

Obviously, these are still "counting interpretations." The phenomena being counted, however, concern the shaman's vision quest, not unrelated matters like moons, suns, solstices or bighorn kills. Even if we cannot interpret the specific Coso dots, it is very likely that they symbolized something closely allied to vision quest practices, because this was the underlying cultural tradition behind the production of the petroglyphs.

PANEL 16: Another interesting panel is located on a large boulder that has fallen away from the cliff and now is on the canyon bottom, on the right side. The panel faces down canyon and is tilted at about a 45 degree angle, so it is hard to see the petroglyphs until you walk past the boulder and turn to look up canyon. The panel contains some complex geometric forms, including a net-like design with a series of parallel wavy lines extending downwards. The most interesting motif, however, is a small elaborate human figure. It is shown upside down (Fig. 21).

By examining the boulder, it is immediately obvious that this panel did not fall off the cliff face, resulting in an inverted human figure. Instead, it appears that this petroglyph was intentionally pecked upside down, and thus matches a number of bighorn motifs in the area that are also inverted, or at least are shown rotated off the horizontal plane that would be standard for "normal" vision. The rotation of images off the horizontal plane is another characteristic of the mental images of a trance, like superpositioning and juxtapositioning, further demonstrating that these petroglyphs are intended to portray supernatural rather than natural events and images.

PANEL 17: A final panel worth noting in this area is located on the right side of the canyon at the end of the gallery, directly above the wire fence and

Figure 21. Upside down human figure

about midway up the canyon wall. This is a line of small stick-figure humans that have been pecked on two faces of the outcrop, wrapping around the corner of this rock exposure (Fig. 22). This linear array of motifs is notable for two reasons, the first of which concerns its content. Verbal accounts of shamans' trances include descriptions of dances and ceremonies, reflecting the belief that the shaman "received" his ceremonies during his visionary

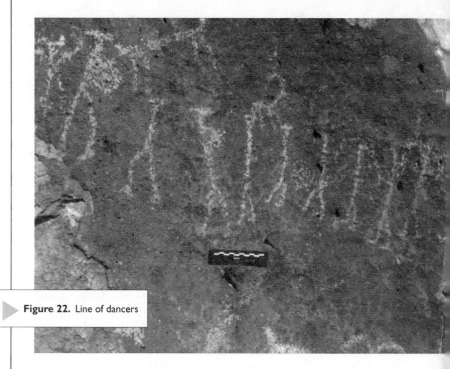

Figure 22. Line of dancers

experiences. Thus, he putatively learned how to conduct his rituals and to lead his dances while in the supernatural realm. Visions of such activities, therefore, logically should appear in the rock art. Similar "dance-line" motifs are known from various Coso sites.

The second notable feature about this panel is the diminutive size of the motifs, at least relative to many other human figures, and especially the elaborate human figure intended to portray the shaman himself. While the size of these figures may be partly for convenience, another characteristic of trance imagery is the perception of small sized hallucinations. These are known as "Lilliputian hallucinations." The small size of these human motifs and many of the bighorns seen in this canyon may be a result of the imagery of trance rather than simply the creativity of the artist.

The gallery at and below Marker K5 is the limit of the major concentration of petroglyphs in Little Petroglyph Canyon. The basalt canyon walls drop off at the southern end of the gallery and, when the walls reappear further south, they comprise a much lower and narrower canyon. While there certainly are some very important panels further on, these are dispersed with much less to see in between. For those interested in continuing on, the distance from Marker K5 to P1 is about 80 yards, P1 to P2 is approximately 100 yards, and P2 to P3 about 35 yards.

▼ Marker P3 to P4

The distance from Marker P3 to P4 is about 45 yards. The petroglyphs are relatively widely dispersed in this area, but those that are present include some exceptional examples. Watch for a nicely rendered human footprint, at eye level on your right, immediately below a low "waterfall" area. Footprints seen in visionary experiences were believed to belong to the "water-baby," one of the shamans' strongest spirit helpers. Visions of a water baby were believed to result in curing power.

PANEL 18: This is located on the right side of the canyon on a rock face that is almost horizontal and that faces down canyon. The canyon wall is very low in this area and this panel is close to the wash bottom.

Another important panel is slightly down the canyon from the footprint, also on the right hand side of the canyon, at about eye level. This contains two bighorns, the upper of which is inverted, impaled with a spear or arrow, and clearly bloated in death (Fig. 23). A clearer representation of a killed sheep cannot be imagined. As discussed in some detail in connection with Panel 10, the "killing of a bighorn" was a metaphor for the Rain-shaman's supernatural acts intended to make rain, using the metaphor of death/killing for entering a trance, and the equivalence of the shaman with his spirit helper. In other words, the dead sheep was the Rain-shaman in the supernatural realm, because his trance was a kind of ritual auto-sacrifice, and because he transformed into a sheep spirit in the sacred realm.

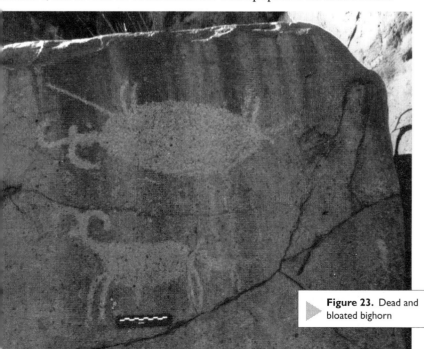

Figure 23. Dead and bloated bighorn

That this symbolism is complex and not obvious might cause some to discount or dismiss it at the outset. This would be a mistake, for the implication of such an attitude is insidious, suggesting doubt that Native American symbolism (and therefore mental capabilities) were not the equivalent of our own in complexity and richness. Such an attitude cannot be supported on biological or cultural grounds. Even though the Native American occupants of this region lacked many of the material cultural trappings of modern societies, we can be certain that their mental capabilities were every bit as rich as our own. After all, they managed to survive quite successfully in one of the harshest environments in North America with little more than their wits. It was their knowledge and therefore mental life that kept them alive in this harshest of landscapes, and we should expect that the mental capacities required for such survival would contribute to a richness in symbolism and belief.

In addition to the killed bighorn motif, a series of more typical "hunter and sheep" motifs are located on the right hand side in this portion of the canyon. Like the majority of such motifs in the Cosos, these are shown with bows and arrows. That the largest proportion of these rain shamanism petroglyphs display weapons that are less than 1500 years old suggests that rain shamanism increased significantly in this region during this period. Why this was so is not entirely understood, but it is known that a debilitating drought affected large portions of western North America about 800 years ago. It may well be that the increase in rain shamanism was partly or primarily in response to the drying of the environment that occurred at that time, and the difficulties this caused for people principally subsisting on plant foods.

▼ MARKER P4 TO P5

The distance between Marker P4 and P5 is only about 40 yards, all of which fall within an increasingly narrow but relatively low-sided portion of the canyon. About 10 yards beyond P4, on your right hand side, is a large vertical panel with a series of "hunter and sheep" motifs, the graphic metaphor for making rain.

PANEL 19: This is located on the right side of the canyon on a rock face that is almost horizontal and that faces down canyon. The canyon wall is very low in this area and this panel is close to the wash bottom.

A large, almost horizontal panel of humans, a bighorn and a variety of entoptics are located just below the "hunter and sheep" panel, but on the left-hand side of the canyon (Fig. 24). This is one of the relatively few panels in Little Petroglyph Canyon that has been vandalized. While disturbing, the graffiti on this panel makes it all the easier to appreciate the generally pristine state of most of the rock art in the canyon, for which we can thank the Navy.

The bighorn, in outline form, is one of the bigger sheep petroglyphs in

Figure 24. Bird shaman etc.

the Cosos. Near it are two elaborate human figures, one of which is particularly interesting. The design on the ritual shirt of this figure starts at the bottom as a solid pecked-out area that breaks up into a random pattern of lines as it moves upwards. More important, though, is the head on this figure — a bird head and beak. As noted previously, birds were strongly associated with shamans, and many of the elaborate Coso human figures combine human and bird characteristics. This was because of the bird's ability to fly. Like the bird (and the whirlwind), the shaman was thought to be capable of flying because of his supernatural power. Birds were common spirit helpers for shamans, and the shaman's ceremonial costume was predominantly made of bird parts. As noted above, the special ritual headgear for the Rain-shaman was a bighorn skin cap sewn with quail topknot feathers. But generally feather headdresses of many kinds were the shaman's headwear for ceremonies. Shamans' ceremonial kilts too were made of feathers, while they used strings of feather-down as ceremonial objects and feather bundles or fans as part of their ritual accouterments.

The putative ability of the shaman to fly while in the supernatural realm has been noted above and warrants some discussion. Like death and killing, flight was a metaphor for entering the supernatural realm that resulted from some of the physical hallucinations and bodily effects of trance. These often included feelings of weightlessness, movement and vertigo; changes in vision making things appear at a distance; and a dissociative mental state that seemed to set the shaman apart from his hallucinations. "Flight" was the Native American metaphor calling upon these reactions to describe the otherwise indescribable experience of going into the supernatural realm. In our own culture we use similar metaphors to describe our trances, based on the same bodily reactions and hallucinations. These include the phrases "going on a trip" and "out of body experience" as ways of quickly describing the effects of a trance.

As should now be clear, the shaman depicted himself as partly transformed into a bird because the ability to fly was one of his defining supernatural powers. We can understand this symbolism partly through Native American commentaries which have explained their beliefs and customs, and also partly because some of the symbolism touches on common cross-cultural reactions to a trance. These reactions are not universal because they touch some deep-seated Jungian or Freudian principles in our brains, whatever these might be. Instead, it is because all humans share the same neuropsychological systems, and therefore react in similar ways in a trance.

▼ Marker P5 to S1

As you move farther down the canyon, the landscape alternates between narrow rocky chutes with low walls, and slightly wider, boulder strewn expanses. The distance from Marker P5 to S1 is short, only about 25 yards. When you get to S1, you will have arrived at one of the most spectacular panels in Little Petroglyph Canyon.

Panel 20: This is located on the right side of the canyon on a rock face that is almost horizontal and that faces down canyon. The canyon wall is

Figure 25. Panel of shaman figures

very low in this area and therefore the panel is close to the wash bottom.

This panel is located at the top of the canyon wall on your right side and faces downstream, so you will have to move a few yards down from the marker to see it clearly. It is a large panel with a series of elaborate human figures, along with a variety of smaller entoptic forms (Fig. 25). As you will immediately see, concentric circles are the common face stylization for these human figures, alluding to the shaman's connection to the whirlwind and therefore his ability to concentrate power and to fly. A number of the shamans' ritual shirts are shown with fringed bottoms, making it clear that these are garments rather than simply the shamans' painted bodies. Two of the human figures are also shown wearing ear ornaments. Although slightly unusual, ear ornamentation was practiced by various western North American groups.

From the archaeological perspective, one of the most interesting aspects of this panel is that some of the motifs appear to have been partially repecked. Judging from the degree of revarnishing within the individual motifs, portions of them were re-engraved at a later date. What this suggests is that Native American shamans not only made their own petroglyphs at the conclusions of their vision quests in the canyon, but also studied and perhaps ritually "renewed" certain older motifs. Similar evidence of repecking has been noted at other petroglyph sites, and certain petroglyphs have been painted over with red pigment, which may reflect this same kind of activity.

Native American accounts provide partial confirmation for this inference. They indicate that individuals wanting to become shamans would come to a vision quest site, select the "spirit" on the rocks they wished to receive, and then pray to and concentrate on that spirit so they would receive its power during their trance. Though no mention is made of repecking or over-painting in this brief account, it is certainly plausible that such activities would also be conducted by the shaman-initiates at this time.

These accounts further indicate that earlier rock art influenced the making of later motifs, an important point since the interpretation of the petroglyphs that has been presented in this guide is derived primarily from historical Native American accounts. How do we know that historical practices and beliefs were also maintained thousands of years earlier, and therefore apply to all of the petroglyphs in the canyon? We cannot prove that the historical meanings of the petroglyphs definitely pertain to older motifs, and thus our projection of these historical meanings and beliefs onto more ancient petroglyphs remains a hypothesis. Still, every line of evidence that we currently have supports this hypothesis, including examples such as this panel. So we believe that there was continuity over time in making and using the Coso petroglyphs.

▼ MARKER S1 TO THE END OF THE CANYON

The distance from Marker S1 to the end of the canyon is about 520 yards, passing Markers S2 through S5 and then T1 through T4. Rock art is sporadically distributed along this stretch, with occasional small concentrations separated by empty zones. As you approach the end, you will see many examples of the kinds of motifs seen upstream in the canyon as well as a number of insect-like motifs near the terminus. These probably represent evil supernatural power or "sickness," which was sometimes conceptualized as "insects".

The end of the canyon is a very dramatic drop off that overlooks the China Lake Basin and Indian Wells Valley, with Ridgecrest far to the south. Be very careful near this drop off. It is a long way to the bottom and you will need the whirlwind power of the shaman to survive a fall.

As you head back up the canyon, you will notice many petroglyphs that you missed on your way down. This is partly because of the changing conditions of the lighting and partly a result of the directions that the different panels face. On your trek back to your car, as well as on your subsequent visits to the canyon, you will quickly realize that there are always new things to see in the canyon.

Native Americans knew this. They said it was because spirits were always making new petroglyphs. Maybe they were right!

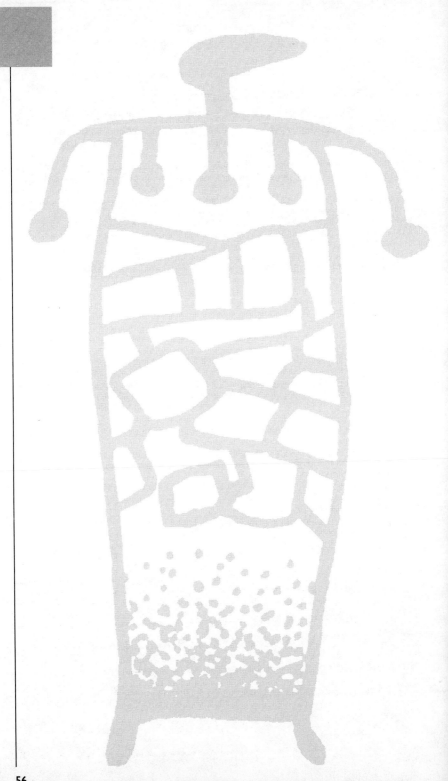

III
FURTHER READING

▼

For those interested in more information on the Coso petroglyphs, the Native American inhabitants of this region, and rock art more generally, the following books are recommended.

Coso Rock Art: A New Perspective, edited by Elva Younkin (Ridgecrest, CA: Maturango Museum, 1998). This book is an up-to-date summary of the dating and interpretation of the Coso petroglyphs, along with the prehistory and ethnography of the Native Americans of this region.

A Guide to Rock Art Sites: Southern California and Southern Nevada, by David S. Whitley (Missoula, MT: Mountain Press Publishing Company, Inc., 1996). This is a guide to 38 rock art sites that are open for public visits, with explanations of the rock art at each.

Shamanism and Rock Art in North America, edited by Solveig Turpin (San Antonio, TX: Rock Art Foundation, Inc., 1994). Monograph comprising five papers showing the links between the rock art of different regions in North America and shamanistic beliefs, practices and symbolism.

Handbook of Rock Art Research, edited by David S. Whitley (Walnut Creek, CA: Alta Mira Press, 1998). This volume summarizes different research techniques used to study rock art, and gives an overview of world rock art, including that of western North America.

New Light on Old Art: Recent Advances in Hunter-Gatherer Rock Art Research, edited by David S. Whitley and Lawrence L. Loendorf (Los Angeles: UCLA Institute of Archaeology, Monograph 36, 1994). This is a collection of technical papers on the dating and interpretation of primarily western North American rock art.

IV
INDEX

INDEX

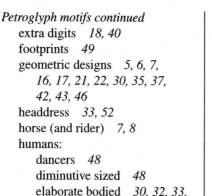

INDEX

Notes

NOTES

NOTES

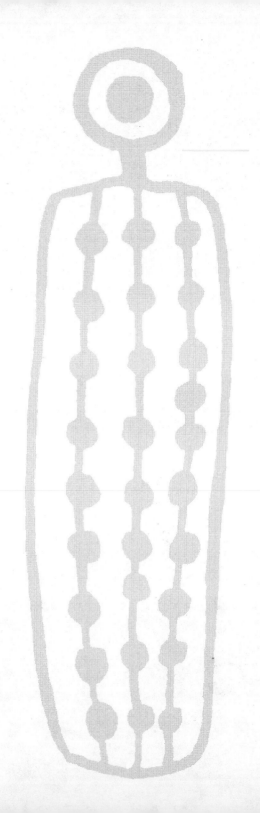